CONTENTS

Some words are shown in bold, **like this**. You can find out what they mean by looking in the glossary.

WHAT WAS WORLD WAR I?

The war that ended on 11 November 1918 was the biggest conflict in human history up to that point. It was the first war that was fought across most parts of the world. Millions of people were killed as fighting spread from Europe around the globe.

Millions of men fought the war from trenches dug across northern France and Belgium.

HOME FRONTS

We call the living conditions and what happens to people not involved in the fighting the "home front" of a country. The lives of millions of men, women, and children on the home fronts were changed forever. World War I was the first global "total war". In a total war, the industry and all the people in a country have to make a contribution to winning the war.

REMEMBERING WORLD WAR I

THE HOME FRONTS IN WORLD WAR I

Nick Hunter

Raintree is an imprint of Capstone Global Library Limited, a company incorporated in England and Wales having its registered office at 7 Pilgrim Street, London, EC4V 6LB – Registered company number: 6695582

www.raintreepublishers.co.uk
myorders@raintreepublishers.co.uk.

Edited by Andrew Farrow, Laura Hensley, and
    John-Paul Wilkins
Designed by Joanna Malivoire and Clare Webber
Original illustrations © Capstone Global Library Ltd
    2014
Illustrated by HL Studios
Picture research by Ruth Blair
Production by Sophia Argyris
Originated by Capstone Global Library Ltd
Printed and bound in China by CTPS

ISBN 978 1 406 26139 4 (hardback)
17 16 15 14 13
10 9 8 7 6 5 4 3 2 1

ISBN 978 1 406 26144 8 (paperback)
18 17 16 15 14
10 9 8 7 6 5 4 3 2 1

British Library Cataloguing in Publication Data
Hunter, Nick.
The home fronts in World War I. -- (Remembering World War I)
940.3'1-dc23
A full catalogue record for this book is available from the British Library.

Acknowledgements
We would like to thank the following for permission to reproduce photographs: AKG Images pp. 5, 7, 15, 27 (ullstein bild), 6, 10, 13, 25, 26, 34, 39, 41; Getty Images pp. 4, 18, 42 (Popperfoto), 12, 14, 17, 19, 20, 31, 35, 36, 38 (Hulton Archive), 22 (Three Lions/Hulton Archive), 28, 29, (Lewis W. Hine/Buyenlarge), 30 (Fotosearch), 32 (Bentley Archive/Popperfoto), 37 (OFF/AFP), 43 (George C Beresford); Mary Evans pp. 23 (© Illustrated London News Ltd), 33 (Robert Hunt Collection).

Cover photograph of refugee children in Poland reproduced with permission of Corbis.

We would like to thank Stewart Ross for his invaluable help in the preparation of this book.

Every effort has been made to contact copyright holders of material reproduced in this book. Any omissions will be rectified in subsequent printings if notice is given to the publisher.

On the home fronts, often far away from the fighting, people had to make supplies to be used by the armies fighting in the war. People on the home fronts also faced direct attacks from **artillery**, aircraft, and ships. Both sides also attacked food supplies and ships bringing food, causing food shortages or even starvation.

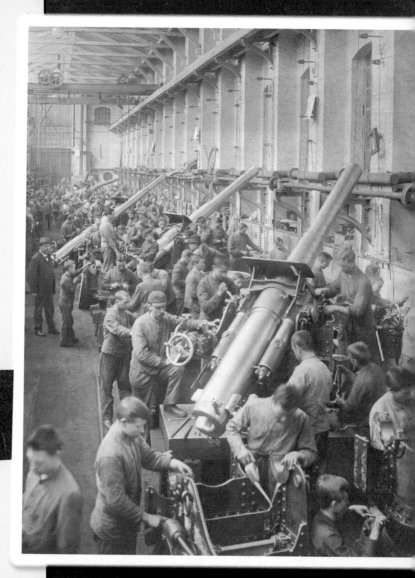

Factories on the home fronts had to make vast quantities of weapons and shells to supply the armies of World War I.

In their own words

"I'd had one year up at Cambridge [University] and then **volunteered** for the army. We were quite clear that Germany would be defeated by the 7th of October, when we would go back to Cambridge."

Private Godfrey Buxton was just one of the many people who expected the war to be a short one

HOW DID PEOPLE REACT WHEN THE WAR STARTED?

At the start of the war, the **Central Powers** of Germany and **Austria-Hungary** were fighting against the forces of France, Russia, Great Britain, and Belgium. Belgium was forced into war when German troops invaded the country to attack France.

WAR FEVER

The outbreak of war was greeted by cheering crowds across Europe. France and Germany expected all young men to serve in the army and could **mobilize** millions of men in a few days. Britain had only a small professional army but, in just a few weeks, half a million volunteers were in training to fight. The major world power outside Europe, the United States, at first adopted a policy of **neutrality**. It would later enter the war in 1917.

The young men who went off to fight in 1914, like these German soldiers, did not know if they would see their homes again.

In the decades before 1914, many wars involving Europeans had been fought in distant **colonies** against much less well-armed opponents. In Europe, Prussia had defeated France in a short war in 1870–1871 on its way to creating the country of Germany. Since then, new technology, such as self-powered machine guns and powerful artillery, had led to major changes in warfare. Excitement would turn to horror as people began to see the effects of these changes.

In their own words

"Crowds gathered at every station, behind every barrier, and at every window along the road. Cries of 'Long live France! Long live the army!' could be heard everywhere while people waved handkerchiefs and hats."

A French officer describes scenes as troops travelled to the front line on thousands of trains

"Let his heart a thousandfold Take the field again!"

ARE **YOU** ONE OF **KITCHENER'S OWN?**

K 244 Q

NOW RECRUITING UNDER Lt. Col. F. M. McROBIE. HIGH SCHOOL BARRACKS. 197 PEEL STREET. MONTREAL.

WHO'S WHO?

Lord Kitchener (1850–1916)

Before 1914, Lord Herbert Kitchener had built his reputation leading British forces in different parts of the British Empire. In 1914, as Secretary for War, he successfully recruited a volunteer army, so British troop numbers increased from 160,000 in August 1914 to more than 2 million in 1915.

THE WARRING NATIONS

Most countries expected the war to be short and that they would end up winning easily. They could not all be right and some countries were much better prepared for a long war than others. However, none were prepared for the brutality and deadliness of modern warfare.

Legend:
- Allies
- Central Powers
- Neutral Countries

0 — 500 km
0 — 400 miles

N W E S

NORWAY
SWEDEN
DENMARK
Baltic Sea
Moscow •
RUSSIAN EMPIRE
BRITAIN
London •
NETHERLANDS
Berlin •
POLAND
BELGIUM
GERMANY
LUXEMBOURG
Paris •
Vienna •
FRANCE
SWITZERLAND
AUSTRIA-HUNGARY
Bordeaux •
ROMANIA
Black Sea
ITALY
BOSNIA
SERBIA
BULGARIA
MONTENEGRO
PORTUGAL
SPAIN
Rome •
ALBANIA
Gallipoli •
OTTOMAN EMPIRE (TURKEY)
GREECE
Mediterranean Sea

The countries of Europe in 1914. Four years of war would change this map forever.

DID YOU KNOW?

The Ottoman Empire was founded by Turkish tribes around the beginning of the 14th century. At its height, it was one of the most powerful empires in the world and covered parts of Europe, Asia, and Africa. It came to an end in 1922 when the monarchy was abolished.

CENTRAL POWERS

Germany had only been a united nation since 1871. However, by 1914 it was undoubtedly the industrial giant of mainland Europe. It had around 50 per cent more people than when it had been formed in 1871. The sprawling empire of Austria-Hungary also had a fast-growing population, but it was struggling to control the people on its borders who wanted independence. Turkey, which joined the Central Powers in late 1914, was also trying to control its large empire in the Middle East.

THE ALLIES

France had been mainland Europe's strongest power before the rise of Germany. It had been weakened by defeat in 1871, and its population had not grown as fast. Britain's main interests lay in its vast empire outside Europe. It could call on soldiers and supplies from **dominions** such as Australia, Canada, and India, as well as its remaining colonies. The country had mainly stayed out of European affairs in the 1800s, but did fear the challenge of Germany. Russia had more people and land than the other powers, but it was held back by poor government, slow progress in industry, and the grinding poverty of many of its people.

In their own words

"It would be **patriotic** ... if the audience in this theater would refrain during the showing of pictures connected with the present war from expressing either approval or disapproval."

US President Woodrow Wilson's message was shown in cinemas in 1914. Wilson was aware that, while many Americans supported the **Allies**, German-Americans in particular did not.

WHY WAS WORLD WAR I A "TOTAL WAR"?

After a few weeks of conflict, it became clear that the war would not be over quickly. By the beginning of 1915, German, French, and British forces were facing each other from **trenches** in northeast France and Belgium. They would barely move from these positions for the next three years, despite many bloody battles. Battles between Russia, Germany, and Austria-Hungary in the East moved faster, but still no country gained a decisive advantage.

Towns and villages close to the front line were shattered by the bombs and shells of the war.

To win the war, every part of society in the warring nations would have to work together in a total war effort. Warships and submarines were used to prevent food and other supplies coming from overseas. New aircraft also created the possibility of attacks on cities far from the fighting.

Georges Clemenceau (1841–1929)

Frenchman "Tiger" Clemenceau understood that winning the war required total commitment. As a journalist and politician, he argued strongly for more soldiers, weapons, and medical supplies. He was called the "Father of Victory" for his leadership of France after he became prime minister in 1917.

GOVERNMENT CONTROL

Governments realized that they needed as much control over what was happening in homes and industries as they did on the front line. In Britain, the Defence of the Realm Act (1914) enabled the government to take what measures it needed to supply and pay for the war, including taking control of railways.

In their own words

"Then we heard that the khaki men [soldiers] were coming to take away all the horses from the village. Everything in the village was done by horses. The milk was collected by horses and the butter used to be collected from the farms and brought in by horses..."

Elizabeth Owen, a British schoolgirl in 1914. Horses were used in the war to move supplies and artillery.

MUNITIONS CRISIS

In their attempts to gain an advantage over the enemy, all armies fired huge quantities of **shells** from their artillery. Germany and France started to run low on shells just a few weeks into the war. In France, 500,000 men were sent back from the front line to work in **munitions** factories that made weapons, guns, bullets, and shells.

Many of the workers in dirty and dangerous munitions factories were women. Some of these women were joining the workforce for the first time. Often they transferred from other factories, such as those making clothes or items for consumers, which were not seen as essential in wartime.

DID YOU KNOW?

By 1916, US goods sold to the Allies were worth 3,000 times the trade with Germany. Much of this trade was in munitions.

Munitions factories could be very dangerous. An explosion at the Silvertown factory in east London destroyed everything within 450 metres (1,500 feet) and claimed 73 lives.

"After each day when we got home we had a lovely good wash… the water was blood red and our skin was perfectly yellow, right down through the body, legs and toenails even, perfectly yellow… Washing wouldn't do anything – it only made it worse."

Mrs M. Hall recalls the effects of working in a munitions factory. The chemicals used in these factories changed the colour of the workers' skin and hair.

SUPPLYING THE FRONT LINE

In addition to munitions, the home fronts had to produce everything else that was needed at the front, from food to boots. Russia showed what could happen when this didn't work. Some Russian soldiers spent long periods without rifles or the clothing they needed to survive harsh winters in the trenches.

German soldiers load up a field train full of supplies, ready for the front line.

13

CARING FOR THE WOUNDED

The sheer number of wounded soldiers in World War I put medical services under great pressure. Wounds caused by bullets and high explosive had to be treated first on the battlefield. Those with serious wounds would be sent to hospitals in their home countries, using specially adapted hospital trains and ships. During the war, several of these ships were sunk by enemy **torpedoes**, including the Canadian HMHS *Llandovery Castle*, in which 234 wounded soldiers, crew, and medical staff died.

Medical staff operate on a wounded soldier in a British military hospital far from the front line.

DID YOU KNOW?

Infection was a major problem. **Antibiotics**, which can stop infections, had not yet been discovered. Even minor wounds could be **fatal** if they became infected.

HOSPITAL TREATMENT

There were not enough hospitals to cope with the numbers of wounded. In Britain, country houses and other buildings were converted into hospitals. Many more women trained as nurses to staff these hospitals. Wounded soldiers had often lost arms and legs or suffered other injuries caused by exploding shells. This led to new techniques for making artificial limbs and surgery to reconstruct faces shattered by shell explosions.

Many of the soldiers who returned to the home front suffered from mental illness as well as physical wounds from their wartime experiences.

In their own words

"The soldiers came straight to us from the boats, on to a train and straight to hospital. Oh, some soldiers were simply dreadful, splattered with blood and dirt and mud. They were still in their khaki, very muddy, very bloody, and terribly, terribly, tired, some very distressed by gas."

British nurse Phyllis Dry remembers casualties arriving at her hospital. Poison gas attacks were used by both sides on the **Western Front**.

DID CIVILIANS FACE ATTACKS?

War also put lives at risk on the home front, although in most cases armies did not deliberately attack **civilians**. People in countries where most fighting took place were threatened much more than those in countries away from the front line, such as Britain and the United States.

This map shows the areas the Allies and Central Powers occupied. The fighting covered a wider area in Eastern Europe. This affected the lives of millions of civilians.

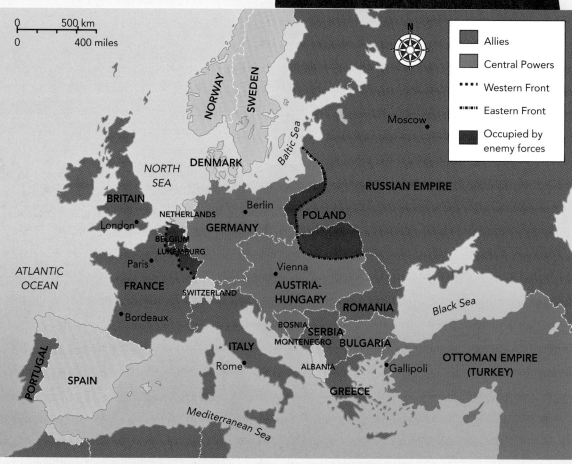

Legend:
- Allies
- Central Powers
- ···· Western Front
- ▪▪▪▪ Eastern Front
- Occupied by enemy forces

0 500 km
0 400 miles

N

NORWAY
SWEDEN
Baltic Sea
Moscow
RUSSIAN EMPIRE
NORTH SEA
DENMARK
BRITAIN
Berlin
NETHERLANDS
London
GERMANY
POLAND
BELGIUM
LUXEMBURG
Paris
ATLANTIC OCEAN
FRANCE
SWITZERLAND
Vienna
AUSTRIA-HUNGARY
ROMANIA
Black Sea
Bordeaux
BOSNIA
SERBIA
MONTENEGRO
BULGARIA
ITALY
PORTUGAL
Rome
ALBANIA
Gallipoli
OTTOMAN EMPIRE (TURKEY)
SPAIN
GREECE
Mediterranean Sea

INVASION AND OCCUPATION

Belgium was invaded by Germany in the first weeks of the war. In order to stop resistance, German forces burned houses and executed many civilians. Many Belgians were moved to Germany and forced to work there. The Serbian population also suffered huge losses in several attacks before Serbia was finally occupied by the Central Powers in late 1915. Fighting in northern France destroyed towns and villages. Lack of food and medical supplies caused hundreds of thousands of deaths in Austria-Hungary and elsewhere in central Europe.

HORROR IN ARMENIA

In some countries, the war provided an excuse for horrific treatment of their own people. Some of Turkey's Christian Armenian subjects sided with Russia in fighting between the two. Turkey used this as an excuse to attack the Armenians. More than 700,000 men, women, and children died as a result.

DID YOU KNOW?

Poland did not exist as an independent country in 1914, but Polish people suffered terribly in the war. When the Russians retreated from Polish land in 1915, they ordered the land to be **evacuated**. Hundreds of thousands of Poles were forced to leave their homes.

COASTS AND SHIPS UNDER ATTACK

Aircraft, airships, and modern warships meant that civilians a long way from the fighting faced new dangers. German warships bombarded British east coast towns, including Whitby and Scarborough, in 1914. These attacks killed more than 100 people.

Anyone who chose to travel overseas faced the hidden threat of German submarines called U-boats. The most famous U-boat attack was the sinking of the liner *Lusitania* with the loss of 1,198 lives, including 128 Americans. Warships and submarines tried to prevent supplies reaching their enemies, causing shortages of food. As early as 1914, Britain set up a Royal Commission on Sugar Supplies to organize sugar supplies from overseas.

The sinking of the *Lusitania* changed many Americans' opinions about entering the war.

W.McDOWELL

AIR ATTACK

Germany used giant Zeppelin airships to bomb cities in Britain and France. Air attack was totally new and terrified those who faced it. Bomber planes were used by all sides, mainly to attack factories and railway stations. Fourteen German Gotha bombers caused 158 deaths in an attack on Britain in June 1917.

In their own words

"The German Zeppelin ... scored a couple of direct hits, causing massive explosions... A few small bi-planes of ours went up to attack it but the Zeppelin had heavy machine-guns mounted in the cabin slung beneath it and, being almost stationary, could take careful aim on a plane... But one little plane went up... Well, this pilot flew above the Zeppelin and dropped bombs onto it... She was on fire all right. Everyone in the street started to cheer."

William Brooks witnesses a Zeppelin raid on London, 1917

Zeppelins moved slowly and, later in the war, aircraft were able to defeat the giant gas balloons with fire-making bullets.

WHAT WAS DAILY LIFE LIKE IN WARTIME?

Europe's people could never escape from the war. It changed almost every aspect of their daily lives. Outside Europe, from Canada to Australia, young men went off to fight in the war. Even in the United States, which did not join the war until 1917, working lives changed as trade in materials, such as cotton, was hit by the war. By contrast, trade boomed in chemicals and raw materials for munitions.

While millions of men went off to fight the war, some jobs were seen as essential for the war effort. Miners were needed to dig for coal and shipbuilding also boomed in Britain.

A large team of workers work closely together to build a ship. Shipbuiliding gained in importance during wartime.

NEW INDUSTRIES

New industries grew during the war, particularly the aircraft industry. Before the war, Germany and France had the most military aircraft with about 1,500 between them. By the time the United States entered the war in 1917, the Allies asked them to provide 4,000 aircraft. In total, more than 200,000 aircraft were produced in the war.

Before the war, men staffed the aircraft factories. Between 1914 and 1918, women took on many of these jobs.

DID YOU KNOW?

Daylight saving time was introduced in Germany, Britain, and the United States in 1916 so that workers could work longer without using power for lighting. Clocks were put forward by one hour in summer.

In their own words

"When mobilization came in 1914, we were midway through the harvest... I had to bring in the grain alone with my fourteen-year-old sister... That year we also had to give up our best horse for war service."

Elise Lohnig had to manage the family farm when her husband joined the German army

FOOD SHORTAGES

Both sides in World War I realized that one of the best ways to defeat their enemies was to stop essential supplies from reaching them by ship. Britain's naval **blockade** reduced German imports by more than half between 1914 and 1915. Food was **rationed** in Germany and Austria-Hungary from 1915, so each household could only buy a small amount. German bread began to include ingredients such as potatoes or even straw as wheat was in such short supply. Around 700,000 people died in Germany due to the effects of starvation and poor **nutrition**.

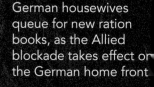

German housewives queue for new ration books, as the Allied blockade takes effect on the German home front

In their own words

"Until 1915 things were just about OK. But then the starvation began. If you had children you received cabbage and some food ... [as rations]. At work, horsemeat and sausages and margarine were handed out. Because I wasn't doing any war work our allowance was very small."

A woman worker recalls food shortages in Berlin, Germany

The British government rationed sugar and meat from 1918, as U-boat attacks stopped supplies coming across the ocean. Rationing made sure that food was distributed fairly and the British people did not face the same crisis as those in central Europe. Any spare land, including parks, was ploughed up to grow food.

In the United States, Charles Lathrop Pack urged Americans to plant war gardens – called victory gardens – so that they could grow enough food for themselves as well as supporting their allies. "Wheatless" and "meatless" days were organized so more food could be sent to soldiers in Europe.

DON'T WASTE BREAD!

SAVE TWO THICK SLICES EVERY DAY, and Defeat the 'U' Boat

Britons were urged to save food by posters like this one.

DID YOU KNOW?

Bread was so rare in Berlin, Germany, that an escaped British prisoner of war was recaptured after he was seen eating a sandwich he had been sent from home.

WAR AND SOCIETY

Maintaining armies was extremely expensive. Prices rose steeply as governments printed paper money to pay for the war. Some business owners – called profiteers – charged extra high prices for items that were scarce. The money that families received while men were away fighting was often much less than they had earned before the war, although these payments actually made some of the poorest families better off during the war.

Governments and volunteer organizations set up soup kitchens to ensure that the poorest people were fed. There were real fears that the strain of wartime shortages and the bad news from the front line might lead to unrest and even **revolution**.

DID YOU KNOW?

There were some unusual responses to shortages. A local council in Kent printed all official papers without punctuation to save paper!

LEISURE TIME

Governments clamped down on anything that might interfere with the war effort. In Britain, all public entertainments had to finish by 10.30 p.m. so workers would not be tired when they arrived at work. Professional sport, including football, was mostly suspended in 1915.

Cinemas became more popular during the war. They were the only places where people could see film of the war, which was heavily **censored** to hide the full horror of the conflict. As coal and other fuels were rationed, cinemas became a place for cold and hungry people to keep warm.

Charlie Chaplin (1889–1977)

Chaplin was the most popular film star of the war years. After becoming a professional entertainer at the age of eight, Chaplin found fame in the United States. In 1918, he made *Shoulder Arms*, in which he played a recruit on a mission behind enemy lines.

CHARLES CHAPLIN
presents
THE CHAPLIN REVUE "U"
"A Dog's Life"—"Shoulder Arms"—"The Pilgrim"
Produced, Written and Directed by
Charles Chaplin
Music Composed by Charles Chaplin

UNITED ARTISTS

WHAT WAS LIFE LIKE FOR CHILDREN?

World War I was a very difficult time for children, even if they lived far from the fighting. In Britain alone, more than 500,000 children lost their fathers during the war. As food shortages became severe, children often went without meals, especially in Germany and Austria-Hungary.

As men left to fight overseas, they were increasingly replaced by women in the workplace. Older children often had to help with caring for younger brothers and sisters at home. For young people whose mothers worked before the war, this was nothing new. Many larger factories now had nurseries where young children could be looked after while their mothers worked.

Families had to live in the knowledge that fathers and brothers may not return from the war.

GOING TO SCHOOL

At school, children were taught patriotic songs and learned about the war. Maps on the wall marked the friendly and enemy countries as well as the sites of major battles. In 1917, US schools put more emphasis on patriotism and supporting the war. Teaching about the war included very little about the true horror of life on the front line, but schoolchildren became used to hearing about the deaths of people they knew.

Refugee camps, like this one in Austria, also made arrangements for schooling.

In their own words

"Sometimes I think the girls keep rejoicing so much [at news of victories] just because they hope there will be a holiday from school. They scream so the headmaster sees what a patriotic school he has, and then perhaps they will be let off the last lesson."

German schoolgirl Piete Kuhr describes her wartime school in eastern Germany

DID YOU KNOW?

In November 1917, schoolchildren in two villages in northeast England went on strike to protest about shortages. They refused to go to school unless they were given free school meals.

HELPING THE WAR EFFORT

By 1918, many children were working for the war effort. Young people could usually leave school in their early teens. There were age restrictions on dangerous work, but still many young people worked in munitions factories. Thousands of underage soldiers claimed to be 18 so they could serve their countries.

In their own words

"10 June 1915: We can hear the noise of artillery. Kids who used to go out with a toy rifle on their shoulder, wearing a red cap with a French flag or a nurse's uniform, are now forbidden to go outside. We are banned from playing soldiers even in our own homes."

Yves Congar was 11 in 1915. He kept a diary of his life in Sedan, France, which was occupied by the German Army during the war.

In the countryside, children had always helped out at busy times of year, such as harvest time. With many farm workers away fighting, and with every scrap of food being important, young people were often given time off school to help in the fields.

In the United States, children were already used to helping with farm work.

Young people's organizations, such as the Boy Scouts and Girl Guides, collected money to help fight the war. In the United States, Boy Scouts raised millions of dollars for the government by selling war bonds. Youth organizations also made bandages or clothing for the soldiers at the front.

LIVING ON THE FRONT LINE

Children faced the everyday danger of living close to the front line, where their lives were disrupted or worse by artillery shells and enemy armies living amongst them. Many became refugees, forced to leave their homes by the war, like the 200,000 Belgians who fled to Britain in 1914.

WHAT DID PEOPLE AT HOME THINK ABOUT THE WAR?

Governments used **propaganda** to control what their people thought about the conflict. Propaganda uses the media to give a particular view of events. At the start of the war, most people supported it. As the war dragged on, it became more important to convince people that it was worthwhile.

A German poster hails the successes of U-boat submarines in sinking enemy merchant ships.

U BOOTE HERAUS!

In their own words

"Wounded and a prisoner, our soldier cries for water. The German 'sister' pours it on the ground before his eyes. There is no woman in Britain who would do it. There is no woman in Britain who will forget it."

An example of the view of Germany promoted on a British propaganda poster

COMMUNICATING ON THE HOME FRONT

With no radio or television, newspapers were the main source of news about the war. Governments tried to control what these papers reported. Public posters were another way of spreading messages to the public. Even famous writers and churches were encouraged to present the government view of the war. These were voices that people listened to and trusted.

Propaganda tried to convince people that it was a good thing to give their time and money to help their country. The enemy was shown to be brutal or evil and so worth fighting against. Government officials called censors also wanted to stop newspapers printing information about war tactics, troop movements, and even details about industry that might help the enemy.

Newspaper sellers bring news of the start of war in August 1914.

DID YOU KNOW?

Robert Goldstein's film *Spirit of '76* told the story of America's War of Independence against Britain in the 1700s. Goldstein was jailed because the cruel British soldiers shown in his film could damage Americans' view of their British allies.

CONSCIENTIOUS OBJECTORS

Germany, France, and most of the warring nations expected all men to serve in the army, so they had millions of soldiers ready to fight in 1914. Britain relied on volunteers until 1916. Those who did not join the military were often insulted or treated harshly for being "shirkers". British women would hand out white feathers to shame men who were not in uniform. In 1916, **conscription** was introduced in Britain, meaning that all men aged between 18 and 41 had to fight.

Conscientious objectors, or "conchies", were people with strong anti-war beliefs, often for religious reasons. If these people could prove their beliefs, they were allowed to do alternative war work, such as working in hospitals or as stretcher carriers in the trenches. A small number of conscientious objectors refused to play any part in the war and were imprisoned. More than 70 conscientious objectors died because of the harsh way they were treated in prison.

Conscientious objectors protest against the war. Only a small minority of people openly campaigned against the war.

"For refusing to be a soldier I am told I may have to forfeit [lose] my life. I cannot understand it. I thought the days of religious persecution were over, and that an Englishman could hold and express his convictions."

Mark Hayler, a British conscientious objector. Hayler was sentenced to hard labour for refusing to fight.

OPPOSITION IN THE UNITED STATES

The United States also introduced conscription when the country entered the war in 1917. Laws were passed to prevent people from criticizing the war. Those who opposed the war, such as 169 leaders of the International Workers of the World, were put in prison.

Some conscientious objectors were imprisoned for their views. These prisoners were forced to do hard labour breaking rocks during the war.

SPIES AND TRAITORS

The authorities and ordinary people had to be on the lookout for those who wanted to help the enemy. The public were warned to be on their guard against spies and **traitors**, and several known spies were arrested in Britain at the start of the war. Anyone who kept homing pigeons that could carry messages had to have a licence. Pigeons were often shot on sight, although this was not officially allowed.

DID YOU KNOW?

On the Allied side, many names were changed to avoid German references. In Russia, the capital St Petersburg became Petrograd. Americans renamed dachshunds as "liberty hounds". In 1917, the British royal family changed its name from the German Saxe-Coburg-Gotha to Windsor.

DER FEIND HÖRT MIT !

VORSICHT BEI GESPRÄCHEN!

This German poster, which roughly translates as "The enemy is listening! Caution during conversations!", was used to warn members of the public about foreign spies.

ANTI-GERMAN FEELINGS

The wave of anger against the enemy meant that innocent people were often caught up in violence. Germans living in Britain were targets. In east London, at least seven Germans were killed in riots after the German sinking of the *Lusitania*. There were similar attacks in the United States, where millions of people were recent immigrants from Germany. They opposed the United States joining the war on the Allied side. Some families changed their names to hide their German origins.

In their own words

"Collinsville, Ill. - April 5, 2 a.m. - Robert P. Praeger, said to be of German parentage, was hanged to a tree one mile south of the city limits here after midnight by a mob of 350 persons. The mob dragged Praeger from the basement of city hall, where he had been hiding. Praeger was accused of making disloyal remarks in a speech he made recently to miners in Maryville, Ill."

Report of the murder of a German-American, from the Chicago Daily Tribune

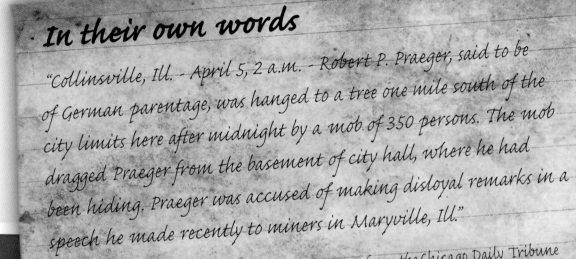

Crowds attack German-owned businesses in London in May 1915.

UNREST AND REVOLUTION

As the war raged, with neither side looking close to victory, governments feared that people would rise up against their leaders. In most cases, these fears did not come true but there was discontent on the home front.

More than 200,000 Irish soldiers fought for Britain in World War I. Before the war, Britain had promised home rule so Ireland would no longer be governed from London, but this had been delayed. Irish nationalists wanted to be independent of Britain. At Easter 1916, they staged an uprising, seizing key buildings in Dublin. The British reacted swiftly, executing the leaders of the rebellion.

Workers in many countries went on strike to protest about shortages. In Britain, France, and the United States, striking workers were threatened with conscription. Elsewhere, governments responded violently. Strikers were shot in Italy and Germany in the later months of the war.

Children collect firewood in the rubble of buildings destroyed during the Easter Rising in Dublin.

Roger Casement (1864–1916)

While many Irish nationalists simply saw World War I as a British conflict that was nothing to do with them, Roger Casement travelled to Berlin to persuade Germany to back a rebellion in Ireland. They refused and Casement returned to Ireland in a German submarine. He was captured by the British and executed for **treason**.

RUSSIAN REVOLUTION

With signs of unrest, governments were worried that their people might follow the example of Russia. In Russia, the disastrous conduct of the war led to a revolution that would change Europe's history for much of the 20th century. It also changed the war as Russia's new leaders made peace with Germany at Brest-Litovsk in March 1918.

Protests against the war and food shortages in the Russian capital Petrograd led to revolution in March 1917.

WHAT HAPPENED AT THE END OF THE WAR?

The fighting finally came to an end on the Western Front on 11 November 1918. After four years of conflict, the Central Powers had been defeated by exhaustion and hunger on the home front as much as by the armies of the Allies. In Russia, World War I was followed by a fierce **civil war** that claimed hundreds of thousands more lives.

By late 1918, people were starving in Germany, and the situation was even worse in Austria-Hungary. In many places, Soldiers' Councils set up by ordinary soldiers, some of whom had deserted the front, were distributing army rations to civilians. The war had cost almost 3 million lives in Germany alone, with millions more wounded. As the people faced defeat, they rebelled against the leaders who had led them into the disastrous war, forcing them to leave power.

A desperate scramble for food at a soup kitchen in Berlin, Germany, in 1918.

In their own words

"The attitude of the German people has furnished the surprise of our lives. Instead of greeting us with dark scowls as hostile foe, they are most cordial and pleasant. I can only account for it by the fact that they are so sick and tired of war and Kaiser [Wilhelm II – the German emperor] that they look upon us more as deliverers ... than as conquerors."

American officer John Clark arrives in Germany in December 1918

SPANISH FLU

The starving people of central Europe lacked coal to keep them warm and soap to keep them clean. These conditions meant they were ill-prepared to face a new threat from a powerful strain of influenza that swept around the world in 1919. The Spanish flu may have claimed 25 million lives, more than the war itself.

Temporary hospitals were set up to treat people suffering from Spanish flu.

LANDS "FIT FOR HEROES"

Britain and France had been victorious in the war, but they could not ignore the huge sacrifices of their people and the changes that the war had brought.

In their own words

"The men and women who looked incredulously into each other's faces did not cry jubilantly: 'We've won the War!' They only said: 'The War is over!'"

Vera Brittain, British author and wartime nurse

Prime Minister Lloyd George promised the British people "a fit country for heroes to live in". Victorian slums were cleared and thousands of new houses built. All men over the age of 21 were allowed to vote in parliamentary elections from 1918. Women were allowed to vote in parliamentary elections for the first time, but not until they were 30. In the United States, returning soldiers were also heralded as heroes. Women were granted the vote in 1920.

TURBULENT TIMES

The years that followed World War I were difficult for many of those who had fought the war on the home front. The years immediately after the war and the 1930s were times of high unemployment and great hardship. Millions of families had to adjust to life without the fathers and sons who had been killed. In 1939, the struggle on the home front began again when the world was plunged into World War II.

A parade under the Washington Square Arch in New York honours the returning American soldiers in 1919.

David Lloyd George (1863–1945)

Before the war, Lloyd George had introduced new **welfare reforms**, such as old age pensions. In 1915, he took charge of the Ministry of Munitions, before becoming Minister of War. He took over as Prime Minister in 1916, leading Britain through the war and the years of reconstruction.

REMEMBERING WORLD WAR I

In the years that followed World War I, memorials were erected across the world. The memorials remember those who did not return home after the war. Many memorials were organized and paid for by local communities, rather than by governments. There are only a few villages in the UK, known as "thankful villages", that have no memorial because all their soldiers returned safely.

People in the victorious countries felt they had won a great victory, although at a terrible cost. Remembering those who had died in the war was very important, and we continue to honour victims of war today, with ceremonies at war memorials around the world.

After the war, memorials were erected on the battlefields where so many lives were lost.

REMEMBERING THE HOME FRONTS

There are few monuments to the home fronts in World War I. There are memorials to those who died in air raids. The day-to-day struggle of the men and women who worked in the factories, suffered food shortages, and cared for the wounded is often forgotten. Yet the hard work of these millions of people was an essential part of World War I and the world that emerged from it.

Art and poetry by war poets like Siegfried Sassoon helped people to understand and remember the horrors of World War I.

In their own words

"I could never understand why my country could call me from a peacetime job and train me to go out to France and try and kill a man I never knew... I didn't discuss the war with anyone from then on and nobody brought it up if they could help it."

Harry Patch, Britain's last surviving Great War veteran, remembers how he felt when he returned home after the war. Patch died in 2009, aged 111.

TIMELINE

1914

28 July–4 August	War is declared, beginning with Austria-Hungary declaring war on Serbia and ending with Britain declaring war on Germany
8 August	Defence of the Realm Act passed in Britain, increasing government control of industry and people
20 August	Britain imposes a naval blockade to prevent supplies reaching the Central Powers

1915

19 January	First Zeppelin raid on Britain, attacks Great Yarmouth on the east coast
April	Ration cards introduced for "war bread" in Austro-Hungarian cities
7 May	Passenger ship *Lusitania* is sunk by German torpedoes, leading to strong anti-German protests in Britain and the United States
23 May	Italy enters the war on the Allied side
9 June	Ministry of Munitions formed in Britain

1916

21 February	Battle of Verdun begins
24 April	Easter Rising in Dublin, Ireland
25 May	Universal conscription introduced in Britain
1 July	Beginning of the Battle of the Somme, with 57,000 British troops killed or wounded on the first day

1917

1 February	Germany declares unrestricted submarine warfare against ships supplying the Allies
March	Charles Lathrop Pack launches his National War Garden Commission in the United States, urging Americans to grow food in their gardens and on unused land
6 April	United States declares war on Germany
May–June	Wave of strikes and unrest across France, alongside mutinies in French armed forces
18 May	President Woodrow Wilson signs Selective Services Act, introducing conscription in the United States
31 July	Battle of Passchendaele, also known as the 3rd Battle of Ypres, begins
10 August	US Food Administration established to manage food supplies and farming
7 November	"October Revolution" begins in Russia, granting power to the Bolsheviks and marking the beginning of Soviet Russia
31 December	Sugar rationing introduced in Britain

1918

January	Strikes and riots in Germany and Austria-Hungary
21 March	German spring offensive begins, pushing Allied forces into retreat
10 June	Representation of the People Act changes British law to allow all men over the age of 21, and women over 30, to vote
11 November	**Armistice** agreed to end fighting on the Western Front at 11 a.m. on the 11th day of the 11th month

GLOSSARY

Allies countries fighting together against the Central Powers, including the empires of France, Russia, and Great Britain, and later the United States

antibiotics medicines that attack bacteria, which cause infection

armistice agreement to stop fighting

artillery heavy guns and cannon, usually moved around on wheels

Austria-Hungary former European monarchy made up of Austria, Hungary, and parts of other countries

blockade use of warships and other means to prevent supplies reaching a country

censor restrict or alter information to prevent people reading or seeing things that may harm them or that officials do not want them to see

Central Powers countries fighting against the Allies in World War I, including Germany, Austria-Hungary, and Turkey

civil war war between citizens of the same country

civilian someone who is not a member of the armed forces

colony land that is ruled or settled by people from overseas

conscientious objector person who refuses to fight for moral or religious reasons

conscription forcing all people in a group, such as all men of a certain age, to serve in the armed forces

dominion self-governing country within the British Empire

Eastern Front border of the territory held by the Central Powers and the Allies, especially Russia, in the East

evacuate move people away from somewhere to keep them safe

fatal causing or likely to cause death

infection when tiny micro-organisms, such as bacteria, enter the body through a wound, for example, and cause further illness

mobilize assemble and prepare soldiers for war

munitions weapons, shells, and other military equipment

neutrality position of not supporting or helping either side in a conflict

nutrition nutrients and energy that we get from eating food

patriotic strongly supporting your own country

propaganda information or art designed to promote a particular view of something, often the view held by the government

rationing restrictions on how much of a product people can buy and use, such as rationing of food in wartime

reform change designed to make things better

refugee person who is forced to leave their home because of war or persecution

revolution overthrow of a government or leader, usually by force, to be replaced by someone else

shell explosive fired from large artillery or cannon

torpedo missile fired underwater from a submarine

traitor person accused of betraying their country

treason crime of betraying one's country

trench ditch dug by soldiers so they can shelter from enemy fire

volunteer freely offer to do something; person who freely offers to do something

welfare services to make people's lives better, such as caring for children and older people

Western Front border of the territory held by the Central Powers and by the Allies in the West, where much of the fighting took place during World War I

FIND OUT MORE

BOOKS

Forgotten Voices of the Great War, Max Arthur (Ebury/Imperial War Museum, 2003)
This book is aimed at adults but includes hundreds of eyewitness stories from the war and the home front.
Men, Women and Children in the First World War, Philip Steele (Wayland, 2012)
My First World War, Daniel James (Franklin Watts, 2010)
World War I (Eyewitness), Simon Adams (Dorling Kindersley, 2011)

WEBSITES

www.anzacday.org.au/history/ww1/homefront/homefront.html
Find out about Australia's home front during World War I.
www.nationalarchives.gov.uk/pathways/firstworldwar
Discover records of life during wartime from the British National Archives.
www.ppu.org.uk/learn/infodocs/cos/st_co_wwone3s3.html
Find out about conscientious objectors and their experiences during the war.
www.spartacus.schoolnet.co.uk/FWWrationing.htm
See the section on rationing in World War I on this history site for schools.

PLACES TO VISIT

Imperial War Museum, London and Manchester
www.iwm.org.uk
Visit the museums to see permanent collections and exhibitions telling the story of war from 1914 to the present day.

Local museums will tell the story of World War I in your area. You may be able to see pictures and read about what people on the home front did to help in fighting the war.

TOPICS FOR FURTHER RESEARCH

- Try to find out more about your own family's experiences of World War I. Although there are few people still alive who lived through the war, you may be able to find photographs or other objects from World War I. Look at old photos of your town between 1914 and 1918.
- Think about how life was different during wartime. Look around your house and school and list the things that you use every day that would not have existed during World War I.
- Pick one of the topics or people covered in this book and research them in more detail. Put together some information and photos to show your class.

INDEX